BREA
DOMINION

Let this book be
a blessing to you.
Much Love
Papa Don Matison

By

APOSTLE DON MATISON

COURSE OUTLINE

Lesson 1
Introduction to Dominion Mandate

INTRODUCTION

Dominion is defined as to lord, to master, to rule over or power to rule, sovereign authority.

Mandate is defined as an authoritative command: a trust.

When we speak of the Dominion Mandate, we speak of God's command to rule, take authority over the earth and everything therein; the land, the sea, the air. The mandate, found in Gen. 1-26-28, was given to Adam and Eve. Adam forfeited his dominion, relinquishing it to Satan, by disobedience to Gods' instructions. Satan convinced Eve that they did not need to listen or to obey God. That which had been forbidden, he promised, would cause them to become as gods, knowing good and evil, when it was eaten. Acting independently of Gods' instructions, they fell into sin and death. They were cut off from their eternal life supply.

Mankind, thereafter, inherited a self-centered nature from his father, Adam. Out of this nature, he attempted to establish dominion and control independent of God's rule and God's life, eating of the same, forbidden fruit, of which Adam and Eve partook. He separates himself from union with God. Until repentance occurs and fellowship is re-established. The world system, governed by the nature inherited from Adam, constantly operates independent of God's authority, because that nature is in rebellion to God.

The Adamic man has within him a basic urge toward dominion, employing it to satisfy his own selfish needs and desires outside of God's authority. It is not an exercise of power under God and to His glory, but a desire to be God. This was exactly the temptation of Satan, that every man should be his own God, deciding for himself what is right and what is wrong.

THE NATURE OF DOMINION

Dominion does not disappear when a man renounces it. It is simply transferred to another person, perhaps to a man's wife, his children, employer, or the state. Where the individual surrenders his due dominion, where the family abdicates it, the workers and the employers reduce it, there's another party, usually the state, concentrates dominion. Where organized society surrenders power, the mob gains it proportionate to the surrender.

Is. 45:18, 19, The earth abideth forever…

Ps. 119:90, God established the earth, it will abide…

Ec. 1:4, The earth abideth forever…

Ps 104:5, Foundation should not be moved forever…

Ps 24:1, the Earth is the Lord's and the fullness thereof…

Clearly, God made the earth and He has a plan for it. His command to His man Adam in the Garden, was to rule the earth, under God. That mandate can be traced down through the pages of history to this present day.

GOD'S PURPOSE IN DOMINION

God's purpose is not the dominion of sinful man, but the dominion of redeemed man, over the earth, under God. Without understanding dominion, God's people have no foundation or authority for movement on the earth. They do not know their right as citizens of God's government on the earth.

As earthly citizens of the United States of America, we have a bill of rights that guarantees each American citizen certain rights. Most of us are familiar with those rights. Many Christians, however, have no idea what their rights are in Jesus Christ. An attitude of relinquishment is in operation in many of the church today. Many false concepts have been embraced by the church which have robbed her of power and authority.

A radical deformation of the gospel and redeemed man's calling crept into the church as a result of Neoplatonism. Neoplatonism was a school of philosophy founded at Alexandria in the third century A.D. It attempted to combine the doctrines of Plato and some other Greek philosophers with the ethical concepts common to Judaism and Christianity, and with the mysticism of the Near East. Dominion was renounced, the earth regarded as the devil's realm, the body despised, and a false humility and meekness cultivated. Dominion was regarded as a burden of the flesh rather than a godly responsibility.

With Pietism, Jesus was pictured as meek and helpless, pacifistic and mild of manner. This led to a false concept of meekness and humility. In the Word of God, the word meek means-

controlled strength in and under God. It speaks of one that has been broken of his own will and made usable in the will of God. Actually, it is one who is under discipline. Moses was the meekest of all men. Anyone looking into the character of Moses, and of Jesus Christ Himself, would have to agree that these men were anything but mousy.

In the scripture, meekness is not the surrender of dominion, but rather the humble and Godly use of dominion. Another way to say *Matt 5:5 is "Blessed are the tamed of God, for they shall inherit the earth."* Another rip-off of God's plan for His people is to believe that the earth belongs to Satan. The Bible clearly shows that the earth is the Lord's and God has a plan continually for it.

GOD'S WILL IN THE EARTH

Gen 1:26-28, And God said, Let us make man in our own image, after our likeness, and let them have dominion over the fish of the sea, and the fowl of the air, and over the cattle and over all the earth, and over every creeping thing that creepeth upon the earth. So, God created man in His own image, in the image of God created He him, male and female, created He them. And God blessed them and God said unto them, be fruitful and multiply and replenish the earth, and subdue it: and have dominion over the fish of the sea, and over the fowl of the air, and over everything that moveth upon the earth.

Every single thing we see around us is made out of the earth. All the animals have a purpose in the plan of God for men. The ocean, the life in the ocean, all has a purpose in the mandate given to Adam to be fruitful, to multiply and replenish the earth, subdue and have dominion.

All food comes out of earth and is transformed into different forms. Grass becomes a cow that produces milk and meat that becomes you. Vegetables, like beans and corn are transformed into a human being as they are eaten and digested, thereby becoming a part of your body. As you eat turkeys on Thanksgiving, the turkey becomes you…ha ha! Everything you see, a skyscraper, a house, a machine, is all transformed dirt. Even the people you see walking up and down the street are made out of the stuff they are walking on. God breathed into the clump of dirt and called him Adam and he became a living soul.

Adam was not Adam before the breath of life. Adam was nothing more than 180 lbs. of dirt;

without life, without personality, without purpose. He was just a lifeless hunk of dirt until God breathed into him His life-giving creative work that created the living soul called Adam. He set him in the Garden of Eden and the fruit of the garden would sustain his body. The Tree of Life in the midst of the garden was actually a representation of the Lord Jesus Christ which would sustain his soul forever.

The second Adam was made a life-giving Spirit. The first Adam ate of the only tree God had forbidden him to eat and he and his wife, Eve, were banished from the garden. They had to sustain their bodies by the sweat of their brow. The earth became hostile, the weather, the animals, all the provisions God had given him, he had to sweat for.

God's plan for man did not change though. His plan still was that man under God would be fruitful, multiply, replenish, subdue and have dominion over the earth. From Adam and Noah, instead of taking dominion, under God, they became totally dominated by their own selfish natures inherited from their forefather Adam. They came under God's judgment. God drowned all of them except Noah and his families and representative animals of every description.

> *Gen 7:1, And the Lord said unto Noah, Come, thou and all thy house into the ark; for I have seen that you are righteous before me int his generation.*

Thus, a new world began with Noah, his wife, his three sons Shem, Ham and Japheth, and their wives, along with animals of all kinds, male and female. God established His covenant with Noah, and as a sign, He put a rainbow in the sky that He would never destroy the earth again by water.

THE DOMINION MANDATE WAS ALSO PASSED DOWN TO NOAH

> *Gen 9:1-2, And God blessed Noah and his sons, and said unto them, "Be fruitful and multiply and replenish the earth. And the fear of you and the dread of you shall be upon every beast of the earth, and upon every fowl of the air, upon all that moveth upon the earth, and upon all the fishes of the sea; into your hand they are delivered."*

The sons of Noah divided the land and to Japheth and sons were divided the Isles of the

Gentiles. The sons of Ham were Cush, Mizriam, Phut and Canaan. Noah cursed Ham for looking on his nakedness while he was drunk. The curse was on Ham and his son, Canaan. His seed would be servants of the others. The cities of Nineveh, Sidon, Sodom and Gomorrah were also built by the descendants of Ham. Nimrod was a grandson of Ham. He was the most popular and greatest warrior and hunter, and also a builder of cities, including Babel.

Shem was the son of Noah that would carry the Godly seed to Abraham, the son of Terah. Before the tower of Babel was built the earth had one language. Man, under Nimrod's leadership, decided to build a tower to reach heaven. God saw that they were of one accord in the natural mind and that nothing they could imagine to do could be withheld. So, God confused the languages and scattered them abroad upon the earth.

ABRAHAM RECEIVED THE MANDATE

In *Gen 12:1-3, Now the Lord had said to Abram, "Get thee out of thy country, and from thy kindred, and from thy father's house, unto a land that I will show thee. And I will make of thee a great nation, and*

I will bless thee, and make thy name great, and thou shalt be a blessing (life Ex 1:13-14), and I will bless them that bless thee, and curse them that curseth thee: and in thee shall all families of the earth be blessed."

About 325 years later, God called Abram (later called Abraham). Abram was from Ur of the Chaldees. He moved from there with his father, Terah, his nephew Lot and Sarai his wife (later called Sarah); to Haran a city named after his uncle. Here is where the dominion mandate is passed down to Abraham, the promise was given. Abraham immediately obeyed God. He gave up all that was precious to him, country, home and friends. Abraham traveled in an unfamiliar land with Isaac, his son of promise. He was tested severely many times. His faith proved that God's call was sure and that he would be called the father of the faithful.

God's promises to Abraham moved on down through Isaac and Jacob (later to be known as Israel). God was raising up a nation to show forth His glory in the earth. God gave the children of Israel, 70 strong, a place of provision in the land of Goshen through the ill treatment of Joseph, one of Jacob's twelve sons, when he was sold as a slave and ended up in an Egyptian jail. Later, he became second in command to the

Pharaoh. During the approximately 215 years of living in Egypt, they multiplied to a nation of three million people.

MOSES WAS GIVEN THE MANDATE

Ex 1:8, Now there arose a new king over Egypt, which knew not Joseph.

After the death of Joseph, the prestige that he and the Israelites held in Egypt gradually ceased to exist. The new pharaoh tried to stop them from multiplying by enslaving them. God saw the bondage that His people were in and He was at work preparing a man for their deliverance. His name was Moses. Moses grew up in the courts of Pharaoh and he was raised as a son of Pharaoh's daughter. God allowed Moses to discover his Hebrew Heritage and as he was observing his people at work, he saw an Egyptian hitting a Hebrew slave. Moses killed him and hid him in the sand. Someone saw this and reported this to Pharaoh. Moses fled from Egypt to the backside of the desert for 40 years. One day, God called Moses and commissioned him to deliver the children of Israel out of slavery, and thus the promise and the dominion mandate were delivered to Moses, as God's representative, to lead the children of Israel.

> *Ex 6:7-8 And I will take you to me for a people, and I will be to you a God; and ye shall know that I am the Lord your God, which bringeth you out from under the burdens of the Egyptians. And I will bring you in unto the land, concerning which I did swear to give it to Abraham, to Isaac and to Jacob; and I will give it you for an heritage, I am the Lord.*

For the first two years, God was leading with a pillar of cloud by day and a pillar of fire by night. After that, God pronounced judgement. They would be wanderers for 40 years. Because of their disobedience and their murmuring, God slew the whole older generation and allowed the younger generation, along with Joshua and Caleb, to enter the land.

Joshua was not the one to carry the promise, to possess the land and take dominion. Through Joshua's leadership, God gave Israel great victories in possessing the land of Canaan, but they failed to rout out all the inhabitants of the land. After Joshua died, there arose a generation that did not know God but served Baal and Ashtaroth.

Judges 2:10-13, And also all that generation were gathered unto their fathers; and there arose another generation after them, which knew not the Lord, nor yet the works which He had done for Israel. And the children of Israel did evil in the sight of the Lord and served Baalim. And they forsook the Lord God of their fathers, which brought them out of the land of Egypt and followed other gods of the people that were round bout them and bowed themselves unto them and they provoked the Lord to anger. And they forsook the Lord and served Baal and Ashtaroth.

During the approximately 300 years of Judges, Israel was in a backslidden condition most of the time. It was time characterization by disunity caused by self-interest and compromise, whenever possible, to avoid war. This led to idol worship. The Lord delivered them into the hands of invading nations but when they cried out to Him, He delivered them. This caused God great sorrow and also anger. The God who delivered them out of bondage, that gave them victory after victory in Canaan, was not fashionable enough for them.

I Sam 8:7-18, And the Lord said unto Samuel, "Hearken unto the voice of the people in all that they say unto thee; for they have rejected me, that

I should not reign over them. According to all the works which they have done since the day that I brought them up out of Egypt even unto this day, wherewith they have forsaken me and served other gods, so do they also unto thee. Now therefore, hearken unto their voice; howbeit yet protest solemnly unto them and show them the manner of the king that shall reign over them." And Samuel told all the words of the Lord unto the people that asked of him a king. And he said, "This will be the manner of the king that shall reign over you; He will take your sons, and appoint them for himself, for his chariots and to be his horsemen; and some shall run before his chariots. And he will appoint him captains over thousands and captains over fifties; and will set them to ear his ground and reap his harvest, and to make his instruments of war and instruments of his chariots. And he will take your daughters to be confectionaries and to be cooks and to be bakers. And he will take your fields, and your vineyard, and your olive yards, even the best of them and give them to his servants. And ye shall cry out in that day because of your king which ye shall have chosen you, and the Lord will not hear you in that day."

They rejected God as their king, so God told Samuel, the last judge of Israel, to let the people have their way and told them of the consequences. The people chose Saul, and the result was failure. Although God honored the peoples' wishes and Samuel's choice, the Spirit of the Lord departed from Saul, because Saul continually disobeyed the Lord.

> *1 Sam 16:14, But the Spirit of the Lord departed from Saul and an evil spirit from the Lord troubled him.*

Saul's forty-year reign is best expressed by his own word. "I have played the fool."

> *1 Sam 26:21, then said Saul, I have sinned; return my son David: for I will no more do thee harm, because My soul was precious in thine eyes this day: behold, I have played the fool and have erred exceedingly.*

During Saul's reign, his disobedience caused God to choose someone else to sit on the throne and rule His people He went to the sheepfold, to a shepherd boy named David, and anointed him king of Israel. God began to move David into a place of prominence that would prepare him to take the throne. David had the opportunity many times to kill Saul and seize the throne, but he let judgement be in the hands of the Lord and Honored God's delegated authority. After Saul's death, David took the throne, and became Israel's greatest king, whose kingdom was a shadow of the kingdom of our Lord Jesus Christ. God passed on the dominion mandate and His promise to his people to David, a descendant of Abraham.

DAVID WAS GIVEN THE MANDATE

> *1 Chron 17:7-15, Now therefore thus shalt thou say unto my servant David, Thus, saith the Lord of hosts, I took thee from the sheepcote, even from following the sheep, that thou shouldest be ruler over my people Israel. And I have been with thee whithersoever thou hast walked and have cut off all thine enemies from before thee and have made thee a name of the great men that are in the earth. Also, I will ordain a place for my people Israel, and will plant them, and they shall dwell in their place, and shall be moved no more; neither shall the children of wickedness waste them anymore, as at the beginning. And since the time that I commanded judges to be over my people Israel. Moreover, I will subdue all thine enemies. Furthermore, I tell thee that the Lord will build thee a house.*

And it shall come to pass, when thy days be expired that thou just go to be with thy fathers, that I will raise up thy seed after thee, which shall be of thy sons: and I will establish his kingdom. He shall build me a house and I will establish his throne forever. I will be his father, and he shall be my son: and I will not take my mercy away from him, as I took it from him that was before thee: But I will settle him in mine house and in my kingdom forever: and his throne shall be established for evermore. According to all these words, and according to all this vision, so did Nathan speak unto David.

From the tribe of Judah, David became the king of Judah first; and seven years later became king of all Israel. David unified Israel and made the country safe from her enemies. He was victorious over the Philistines, Edomites, Moabites, Ammonites and Syrians: and ruled over the whole promised land. David, though being a mighty military man, was a poet and song writer and had a great heart for God. After building a palace for himself he was anxious to build a house for God. God forbade it and told him that his son would build the temple. God told David that He would build him a house and his throne would be established forever.

Israel never forgot God's everlasting covenant with David; they knew for certain that the Messiah would be a son of David. God began to fulfill His promise by setting Solomon on the throne. During his reign, Israel reached the height of its magnificence. Solomon began his reign in fellowship with God, seeking His wisdom and honoring Him. God prospered him. He became the richest man that ever lived. As Solomon progressed, he married many princesses from neighboring nations for different reasons, mostly political. They turned his heart from Jehovah and caused him to worship other gods. He began to oppress the people with high taxes and forced labor. This was the root cause for the divided kingdom under his son Rehoboam: who listened to the advice of young inexperienced counselors instead of the wisdom of the older men. As a result, the ten northern tribes separated themselves from David's dynasty.

Saul, David, and Solomon all reigned 40 years each. From 1050 – 930 B.C. there was a United Kingdom, a period of 120 years.

Jeroboam, one of Solomon's servants and head of his labor force became king of the northern kingdom whose capital city was Shechem (later

Samaria). The northern kingdom lasted approximately 200 years with many changes of kings until Samaria was destroyed in 722 B.C. by the Assyrian King Shalmaneser V. The history of the northern kingdom was marked by disobedience and rebellion against God and the worship of false gods that finally led to their destruction.

Judah, under Rehoboam, was scarcely better, for along with the worship of Jehovah, the people corrupted themselves with some of the abominations of the Canaanite fertility gods. After reigning four or five years, Jerusalem was invaded by Egyptian King Shishah, who stripped the temple of the gold that Solomon had put there. Most of the 275 yeas of rule, by kings of Judah, was also marred by disobedience, rebellion and idolatry.

In 586 B.C. Judah was taken by Nebuchadnezzar of Babylon as Jeremiah the prophet foretold. He said Judah would serve Babylon for 70 years. After this Daniel foretold Babylon's downfall saying, Thy Kingdom is divided and given to the Medes and Persians, Dan 5:25, 31. Darius, the Mede, divided the kingdom in 120 and presided over them. When Cyrus took the throne of Babylon, he issued two decrees authorizing the

Jewish exiles to return home and to rebuild their temple. This was the third act of sovereign mercy of God toward His covenant people. He brought Abraham from Mesopotamia, the 12 tribes out of Egypt, and the exiles from Babylon. Not all came out of Babylon, a large number remained. The book of Esther tells of some of them during the reign of Ahasuerus (Xerses I) who ruled Persia from 486 – 465 B. C. Restoration took place in three stages. First, Zerubbabel left to restore the temple (538 B.C.); Ezra was (445 B.C.) to restore the wall. The work on the temple began in the year 520 B.C. and was finished in 515 B.C. Nearly 75 years later the reconstruction of Israel's' national life began. This was led by Ezra, who was a priest and a scribe. He was sent to Jerusalem by Persian King Artaxerxes in 465 B.C. He was sent to regulate Israel's religious and moral responsibilities in accordance with the law. Thirteen years later Nehemiah was sent by Artaxerxes, to rebuild the city and in particular, the walls.

After opposition and threats the wall was completed and dedicated. During this time national sins were confessed, and the people renewed their covenant with God. Unfortunately, not all reforms undertaken by the people, during the reformation, were kept. When Nehemiah returned, he found several irregularities, such as failure to pay tithes, keep Sabbaths and avoid intermarriage with the heathen. But Nehemiah dealt faithfully with these matters according to God's law. During the next 400 years no book was written. The voice of prophecy was known to be silent. In 331 B.C. Alexander the Great defeated the Persian army. In the height of this military career, Alexander died. His empire was divided into four major regions under his generals Macedonia, Greece, Thrace or West Asia. Syria and Babylonia (and Scleucus) and Egypt (Ptolemy). For the next 300 years, Judea was dominated by the Scleucus (Syrian-Babylonia) and the Ptolemy (Egypt) first the one then the other.

By 198 B.C., the Seleucids had become the stronger kingdom. In 175 B.C. Antiochus IV took the throne of Syria. This man was a wicked ruler that ravaged the Jews. In three days, he killed 80,000 men, women and children; he desecrated the temple by sacrificing unclean animals on the altar. At once resistance broke out and centered around an old priest named Manhattan. After his death, his 5 famous sons began the nucleus of the resistance. The eldest, Judas became the leader, which they named Maccabee (the Hammer). For three years guerrilla war was waged and the little army recaptured Jerusalem and rededicated the temple to the glory of God. The war continued, the reason for war grew to be less for religious freedom and more for national independence. For a short season, Israel became an independent nation in 142 B.C. The little nation from 104 B.C. onward suffered desperately at the hands of a number of ferocious rulers. Finally, it lost its independence in 63 B.C. to the great new rising power of Rome.

Lesson 1 Assignments

LESSON 1 ASSIGNMENT 1

Write about what you learned in the first lesson. Does it seem that the Dominion Mandate may have lost its emphasis in our day and age? Do you have any views or teachings that are contrary to this teaching that you may need to reconsider? What can you take away from this lesson to apply to some specific areas in your life?

LESSON 1 ASSIGNMENT 2

Write out a SMART goal for some specific areas in your life where you would like to increase in boldness and start walking in the Dominion Mandate.

Lesson 2 Jesus Demonstrates the Dominion Mandate

INTRODUCTION

From Genesis to Revelation, Jesus Christ is woven into every book. He is the beginning and the end. The One who stands behind all history, and all things visible and invisible culminate in Him.

> *Col 1:16-17, For by Him were all things created, that are earth, visible and invisible, whether they be thrones, or dominions or principalities, or powers: all things were created by Him and for Him. And He is before all things and by Him all things consist.*

> *Rev. 19:10, For the testimony of Jesus is the spirit of prophecy.*

The place of rule that Jesus Christ was destined to occupy was the very throne of God. The earthly shadow of that throne and the kingdom that it ruled was the Throne of David. The following prophetic passages demonstrate this truth.

DAVID'S THRONE AND HOW IT RELATES TO THE RULE OF THE LORD JESUS CHRIST

This relationship was revealed through God's covenant with David.

> *II Sam 7:9-17, And I was with thee withersoever thou wentest, and have cut off all thine enemies out of thine sight, and have made thee a great name, like unto the name of the great men that are in the earth. Moreover, I will appoint a place for my people Israel, and will plant them, that they may dwell in a place of their own and move no more; neither shall the children of wickedness afflict them anymore, as before time.* And as since the time that I commanded judges to be over my people Israel and have caused thee to rest from all thine enemies. Also, the Lord telleth thee that he will make thee a house. And when thy days be fulfilled, and though shalt sleep with thy fathers, I will set up thy seed after thee which shall proceed out of thy bowels and I will establish His kingdom. He shall build a house for my name, and I will establish the throne of his kingdom forever. I will be his father and he shall be my son. If he commits iniquity, I will chasten him with the rod of men and with the stripes of the children of men. But my mercy shall not

> depart away from him as I took it from Saul, whom I put away before thee. And thine house and thy kingdom shall be established forever before thee; thy throne shall be established forever. According to all these words, and according to all this vision, so did Nathan speak unto David.

This covenant declares that the house, the kingdom and the throne of David would be established forever.

EARTHLY THINGS THAT HAVE HEAVENLY SIGNIFICANCE

House of David – those that came out of him: His offspring, his lineage, his seed

Kingdom of David – the domain of David; that which is under his rule, his territorial rights

Throne of David – David's place of rule; position of rest; resting in his established authority

Zion – A fortress captured by David

GOD'S ETERNAL KINGDOM, GOD'S GOVERNMENT IN THE EARTH

> *II Sam 5:6-9, And the king and his men went to Jerusalem unto the Jebusites, the inhabitants of the land; which spake unto David saying, "Except though take away the blind and the lame thou shalt not come in hither – thinking David cannot come hither." Nevertheless, David took the stronghold of Zion; the same is the city of David.* And David said on that day, whatsoever getteth up to the gutter and smiteth the Jebusites, and the lame and the blind, that are hated of David's own soul. He shall be chief and captain. Wherefore they said, "The blind and the lame shall not come into the house." So, David dwelt in the fort, and called it the city of David. And David built roundabout from Millo and inward.

DAVID'S THRONE TO BE OCCUPIED BY THE MESSIAH

Isaiah's Testimony

> *Is 9:6-8, For unto us a child is born, unto us a son is given; and the government shall be upon his shoulders, and His name shall be called Wonderful, Counselor, The Mighty God, The*

Everlasting Father, The Prince of Peace. Of the increase of his government and peace there shall be no end, upon the throne of David and upon his kingdom to order it and to establish it with judgement and with justice from henceforth even forever. The zeal of the Lord of Hots will perform this.

Luke 1:31-33, And behold, thou shalt conceive in thy womb and bring forth a son and shall call his name Jesus. He shall be great and shall be called the Son of the Highest; and the Lord God shall give unto him the throng of his father David. And he shall reign over the house of Jacob forever and of His Kingdom there shall be no end.

GOD THE FATHER'S TESTIMONY

Matt 3:17, And lo a voice from heaven saying, "This is my beloved Son, in whom I am well pleased."

DOMINION MANDATE TO JESUS

Ps 8:4-9, What is man that thou art mindful of him, and the Son of man that thou visiteth him? For thou hast made him a little lower than the angels, and hast crowned him with glory and honor. Thou made him to have dominion over the works of thy hands; thou hast put all things under his feet. All sheep and oxen, yea, and the beasts of the field; the fowl of the air and the fish of the sea and whatsoever passeth through the paths of the sea. O Lord our Lord, how excellent is thy name in all the earth!

JESUS DEFEATS ALL HIS ENEMIES

Heb 2:6-13, But one in a certain place testified saying, "What is man, that thou art mindful of him? Or the son of man that thou visiteth him?" Thou madest him a little lower than the angels; thou crownedst him with glory and honor, and didst set him over the works of thy hands. Thou hast put all things in subjection under his feet. For in that he put all in subjection under him, he left yet all things put under him. But we see Jesus, who was made a little lower than the angels for the suffering of death, crowned with glory and honor, that he by the grace of God should taste death for every man. For it became him, for whom are all things, and by whom are all things, in bringing many sons unto glory, to make the captain of their salvation perfect through sufferings. For both he that sanctifieth and they who are sanctified are all of one; for which cause, he is not ashamed to call them brethren. Saying, I will declare thy name unto my brethren in the midst of the church will I sing praise unto thee. And again, I will put my trust in him. And again, Behold I and the children which God has given me.

Jesus tasted death for every man. He suffered for mankind. He was raised up as King over all the works of God's hand. He was crowned with glory and honor. He sat down at the right had of the Majesty on high.

Heb 1:3, Who being the brightness of his glory, and the express image of his person, and upholding all things by the word of his power when he had by himself purged our sins, sat down on the right hand of the Majesty on high.

Eph 1:21-23, He was raised far above all principalities and powers, and might and dominion, and every name that is named not only in this world, but also in that which is to come; and hath put all things under his feet, and gave him to be head over all things to the church, which

> *is his body, the fullness of him that filleth all in all.*

To realize the purpose of God in the recovery of all things to Himself and the restoration of what was lost in Adam, there had to be a man, a seed of the earth, of human nature, the seed of Abraham.

> *Heb 2:14-16, Forasmuch then as the children are partakers of flesh and blood, he also himself likewise took part of the same; that through death the might destroy him that had the power of death, that is, the devil, And deliver them who through fear of death were all their lifetimes subject to bondage. For verily he took not on him the nature of angels; but he took on him the seed of Abraham.*

This man was to meet the demands of divine justice, to die the death that was the wage of mankind's and Adam's sin. He was to defeat death by dying and resurrecting from the dead, thereby rendering powerless him who had authority over death, that is the devil, setting at liberty all those who through the fear of death had been subject to lifelong slavery.

> *Heb 2:14-15, Forasmuch then as the children are partakers of flesh and blood, he also himself likewise took part of the same; that through death*

he might destroy hm who had the power of death that is the devil; and deliver them who through fear of death were all their lifetime subject to bondage.

Jesus was that man! He defeated hell, death and the grave. He is seated in the heavenlies, the head of the church, the completeness of Him who fills the universe with Himself.

Eph 1:23, which is his body, the fulness of him that filleth all in all.

Jesus has raised us, who were once dead in trespasses and sins, to a position of ultimate authority over the work s of God's hands. He has raised us to his throne to site with him in the rest of authority, to execute the divine mandate to subdue the enemies of Christ under our feet.

JESUS VICTORY WAS IN HELL, EARTH AND THE HEAVENS

PETER'S SERMON: HELL

Acts 2:24-35, Whom God hath raised up, having loosed the pains of death because it was not possible that he should be holden of it. For David speaketh concerning him, I foresaw the Lord always before my face, for he is on my right hand that I should not be moved. Therefore, did my heart rejoice, and my tongue was glad moreover also my flesh shall rest in hope. Because thou wilt not leave my soul in hell, neither wilt thou suffer thine Holy One to see corruption. Thou hast made known to me the ways of life; thou shalt make me full of joy with thy countenance. Men and brethren let me freely speak unto you of the patriarch David, that he is both dead and buried, and his sepulcher is with us unto this day. Therefore, being a prophet, and knowing that God had sworn an oath to him, that of the fruit of his loins, according to the flesh, he would raise up Christ to sit on his throne. He, seeing this before spake of the resurrection of the Christ, that his soul was not left in hell, neither his flesh did see corruption. This Jesus hath God raised up whereof we all are witnesses. Therefore, being by the right hand of God exalted and having received of the Father the promise of the Holy Ghost he hath shed forth this, which we now see and hear. For David is not ascended into the heavens' but he saith of himself, The Lord said unto my Lord, Sit thou on my right hand, until I make thy foes thy footstool.

EARTH

WILDERNESS TEMPTATION

Matt 4-1-11, Then was Jesus led up of the Spirit unto the wilderness to be tempted of the devil. And when he had fasted forty days and forty nights, he was afterward a hungered. And when the tempter came to him, he said, "If thou be the Son of God, command that these stones be made bread." But He answered and said, "It is written, Man shall not live by bread alone, but by every word that proceedeth out of the mouth of God." Then the devil taketh Him up into the Holy City and setteth Him on a pinnacle of the temple, and saith unto Him, If thou be the Son of God, cast thyself down; for it is written, He shall give His angels charge concerning thee; and in their hands they shall bear thee up lest at any time thou dash thy foot against a stone." Jesus said unto him, "It is written again, thou shalt not tempt the Lord thy God." Again, the devil taketh him up onto an exceeding high mountain and sheweth Him all the kingdoms of the world and the glory of them, and saith unto Him, "All these things will I give thee, if thou wilt fall down and worship me." Then saith Jesus unto him, "Get thee hence, Satan! For it is written, "Thou shalt worship the Lord thy

God and Him only shalt thou serve." Then the devil leaveth Him and behold, angels came and ministered unto him.

GETHSEMANE

Matt 26:36-39, Then cometh Jesus with them unto a place called Gethsemane and saith unto the disciples, "Sit ye here, while I go and pray yonder." And he took with him Peter and the two sons of Zebedee and began to be sorrowful and very heavy. Then saith He unto them, "My soul is exceedingly sorrowful even unto death; tarry ye here and watch with Me." And He went a little farther and fell on His face and prayed, saying, "O My Father, if it be possible, let this cut pass from me; nevertheless, not as I will but as thou wilt."

HEAVENLIES

1. Forgave us of all transgressions.
2. Cancelled the bond (the law) and nailed it to His cross.

3. Stripped hostile princes and rulers from Himself and boldly displayed them as His

conquests when by the cross He triumphed over them.

Col 2:13-15, And you being dead in your sins and uncircumcision o your flesh hath he quickened together with him, having forgiven you all trespasses, blotting out the handwriting of ordinances that was against us, which was contrary to us and took it out of the way, nailing it to His cross. And having spoiled principalities and powers, He made a shew of them openly, triumphing over them in it.

ALL POWER IS GIVEN TO HIM IN HEAVEN AND IN EARTH

Matt 28:18, So we have the authority to go and preach this gospel of the kingdom to the nation.

Ps 2:6, 8, Yet have I set my king upon my holy hill of Zion. I will declare the decree: the Lord hath said unto me, "Thou art My Son; this day have I begotten thee. Ask of Me and I shall give thee the heathen nations) for thine inheritance and the uttermost parts of the earth for thy possession."

It's from this heavenly throne that Jesus rules through the church, His body, until all enemies are put under our feet and we see all enemies there.

> *Ps 110:1, 2, The Lord shall send the rod of thy strength out of Zion: Rule thou in the midst of thine enemies.*

HEAVEN MUST RECEIVE HIM UNTIL

Until the full recovery of all things spoken in ancient times by all His holy prophets.

> *Acts, 3:19-26, Repent ye therefore, and be converted, that your sins may be blotted out, when the times of refreshing shall come from the presence of the Lord, and He shall send Jesus Christ, which before was preached to you. Whom the heaven must receive until the times of restitution of all things, which God hath spoken by thy mouth of all His holy prophets since the world began. For Moses truly said unto the fathers, "A prophet shall the Lord your God raise up unto you of your brethren, like unto me; Him shall ye hear in all things whatsoever He shall say unto you. And it shall come to pass that every soul, which will not hear that prophet, shall be destroyed from among the people. Yea, and all the prophets from Samuel and those that follow after, as many as have spoken, have likewise foretold of*

these days. Ye are the children of the prophets and of the covenant which God made with our fathers, saying unto Abraham. 'And in thy seed shall all the kindreds of the earth be blessed." Unto you first God, having raise up His Son Jesus, sent Him to bless you in turning away every one of you from his iniquities."

I Cor 15:20-28, But now is Christ risen from the dead, and because the first fruits of them that slept. For since by man came death, by man came also the resurrection of the dead. For as in Adam all die, even so in Christ shall all be made alive. But every man in his own order: Christ the first fruits; afterward they that are Christ's at His coming. Then cometh the end, when He shall have delivered up the kingdom to God, even the Father, when we shall have put down all rule and all authority and power. For He must reign, till He hath put all enemies under His feet. The last enemy that shall be destroyed is death. For He hath put all things under His feet. But when He saith all things are put under Him, it is manifest that He is expected, which did put all things under Him. And when all things shall be subdued unto Him, then shall the Son also Himself be subject unto Him that put all things under Him, that God may be all in all.

These scriptures indicate that Jesus Christ must reign in the heavens until God through the Holy Spirit in His body, the church puts all things under His feet, the last enemy that shall be destroyed is death.

How does Jesus Christ who is seated on His heavenly throne rule and subdue the earth? By the Holy Spirit He promised. Upon being exalted to the right hand of God. He received the promise of the Holy Spirit and sent Him into the earth to bear witness through the church that Jesus had ascended. It is His work in the earth that will subdue all things under the feet of Christ. The agency that will do it will be us, the Church!!!

Assignments

LESSON 2 ASSIGNMENT 1

What examples did Jesus give us in walking in Dominion in the Earth? Did He fulfill the Dominion Mandate? In what ways?

LESSON 2 ASSIGNMENT 2

Through this lesson, have you noticed some parallels to Jesus's mandate and our mandate in the earth? What similarities are there and what must we do to walk in this dominion mandate as Jesus did? How can you apply this to your own SMART goals?

Lesson 3
The Family, A Vehicle of Dominion

INTRODUCTION

The family is one of God's main vehicles to take dominion over the earth and subdue it. Its unique order in God Shows His kingdom rule in the earth. It is the ministry of the family in God that subdues our flesh and brings us into obedience to His Word. A Christian marriage is God's visual aid to show forth the relationship between Christ and His church. Eph 5:22-33

THE FAMILY, HUSBANDS AND WIVES

Marriage is a 100% proposition for both partners. Husbands give 100% of themselves under Christ to their wives and the wife gives 100% submission to her husband. They both operate in the realm of authority and submission Christ has delegated to them as husband and wife. Let's take a look at His plan.

> *In the beginning, Gen 2:7, And the Lord God formed man of the dust of the ground and breathed into his nostrils the breath of life; and man became a living soul.*

And God gave to man His ministry, Gen 2:15, and the Lord God took the man and put him into the Garden of Eden to dress it and to keep it.

GOD PROVIDES A HELP FIT FOR HIM

> *Gen 2:18-23, And the Lord God said, It is not good that the man should be alone; I will make him an help meet for him. And out of the ground the Lord God formed every beast of the field, and every fowl of the air, and brought them unto Adam to see what he would call them; and whatsoever Adam called every living creature, that was the name thereof. And Adam gave names to all cattle, and to the fowl of the air, and to every beast of the field; but for Adam thee was not found a help meet for him. And the Lord God caused a deep sleep to fall upon Adam and he slept; and he took one of his ribs and closed up the flesh instead thereof; and the rib which the Lord God had taken from man, made he a woman, and brought her unto the man. And Adam said, "This is now bone of my bones and flesh of my flesh; she shall be called Woman, because she was taken out of Man."*

Adam given prerogative to name every living creature, God gave His stamp of approval

Out of the whole creation, thee was not a help fit for him

God took woman out of man's body to provide help for him in God's purposes for him. Therefore, God was the author of man, and God created woman out of man. Woman's reason for being was found in man. If she were to be a separate entity, God would have taken her out of the earth also…like the other creatures He created.

God authorizes man for His purposes. Man's purposes in God authorizes woman. Man and woman authorize children. This is the principle of authority in the family.

HUSBANDS UNDER LORDSHIP

Marriage, in the kingdom of God, is a far cry from the world's idea of marriage. When God institutes something, He wires it to work. Because He is Lord of what He institutes, He causes it to work when we submit to His principles in marriage. When we, through our own opinion, usurp His order, the marriage short circuits and the power begins to drain off. More natural mind opinion results in a total takeover and the marriage becomes God's enemy. It no longer is run by His mind revealed through His orderly principle but rather the natural mind authorized by human understanding. How can we expect God's blessing when we go contrary to His established order?

As husbands subject themselves to the Lord Jesus, they experience their position in their marriages. What is the husband's position? He learns to rule as he is being ruled by the Lord Jesus. He will exercise Lordship. He will rule. He will be her head.

> *Gen. 3:16, Unto the woman He said, "I will greatly multiply thy sorrow and they conception; in sorrow thou shalt bring forth children; and thy desire shall be to thy husband, and he shall rule over thee".*

As man and wife operate in divine order, it confirms the wisdom of God and glorifies Him that His way was and is the only way.

> *Eph 5:22-24, Wives, submit yourselves unto your own husbands, as unto the Lord. For the husband is the head of the wife, even as Christ is the head of the church; and He is the savior of the body. Therefore, as the church is subject unto Christ, so let the wives be to their own husbands in everything.*

Eph 2:1-2 speaks of the governing system of this world contrived by the natural mind under the control of the spirit that governs the children of disobedience. And you hath He quickened, who were dead in trespasses and sins. Wherein time past ye walked according to the course of this world, according to the prince of the power of the air, the spirit that now worketh in the children of disobedience.

Not only is God glorified and His wisdom confirmed to the world, but also the angels and principalities and powers.

1 Cor 11:9-10, Neither was the man created for the woman; but the woman for the man. For this cause ought the woman to have power on her head because of the angels.

This is the reason for your marriage: to glorify God in God's order for God's purposes.

HUSBANDS LOVE YOUR WIVES

Eph 5:25, Husbands, love your wives, even as Christ also loved the church and gave Himself for it. That He might sanctify and cleanse it with the washing of water by the word, that He might present it to Himself a glorious church, not having spot or wrinkle, or any such thing; but that it should be holy and without blemish. So, ought men to love their wives as their own bodies. He that loveth his wife loveth himself.

When we consider Christ's love for us, we notice that it was self-sacrificial – He died for us. He paid the price and what a price! EVERYTHING!!! As husbands submit themselves to the Lord Jesus, their head, they experience His love in many ways.

IN COMFORT

2 Cor 1:3-5, Thank God, the Father of our Lord Jesus Christ, that He is our Father and the source of all mercy and comfort. For He gives us comfort in all our trials so that we in turn may be able to give the same sort of strong sympathy to others in their troubles. Indeed, experience shows that the more we share in Christ's immeasurable suffering, the more we are able to give of His encouragement.

CHASTENING

Heb 12:4-13, After all, your fight against sin has not yet meant the shedding of blood, and you have perhaps lost sight of that piece of advice which

> *reminds you of your sonship in God: My son regard not lightly the chastening of the Lord, nor faint when thou art reproved of Him; For whom the lord loveth He chastenest, and scourgeth every son whom He receiveth.*

Bear what you have to bear as "chastening" as God's dealing with you as sons. No true son ever grows up uncorrected by his father. For if you had no experience of the correction which all sons have to bear, you might well doubt the legitimacy of your sonship. After all, when we were children, we had fathers who corrected us, and we respected them for it. Can we not much more readily submit to the discipline of the Father of men's souls and learn how to live?

For our fathers used to correct us according to their own ideas during the brief days of childhood. Bur God corrects us for our own benefit, so that we may share in His holiness. Now obviously, no chastening seems pleasant at the time; it is in fact, most unpleasant. Yet when it is all over, we can see that it has quietly produced the fruit of real goodness in the characters of those who have accepted it. So, tighten your loosening grip and steady your trembling knees. Keep your feet on a steady path, so that the limping foot does not collapse but recovers strength.

TRIALS AND SUFFERING

Rom 5:1-5, Therefore, now that we have been justified through faith, let us continue at peace with God through our Lord Jesus Christ, through whom we have been allowed to enter the sphere of God's grace, where we now stand. Let us exalt in the hope of the divine splendor that is to be ours. More than this, let us even exalt in our present sufferings, because we know that the suffering trains us to endure, and endurance brings proof that we have stood the test, and this proof is the ground of hope. Such a hope Is no mockery, because God's love has flooded our inmost heart through the Holy Spirit, He has given us.

REBUKE

Rev 3:19, I continually discipline and punish everyone I love; so, I must punish you, unless you turn from your indifference and become enthusiastic about the things of God.

FRUIT OF THE SPIRIT

Gal 5:22-23, The Spirit, however, produces in human life, fruits such as these; love, joy, peace, patience, kindness, generosity, fidelity, tolerance and self-control – and no law exists against any of them.

SO, OUGHT MEN TO LOVE THEIR WIVES

I Pet 3:7, Similarly, you husbands should try to understand the wife you live with, honoring them as physically weaker, yet equally heirs with you of the grace of life. If you don't do this, you will find it impossible to pray together properly.

Husbands should understand their wives in the Lord and honor them as the physically weaker vessel. Realizing that the Lord loves them just as much as He does the husband; His blood was shed for them. He gave the wives as a gift and help. God created Eve and gave her to Adam.

Husbands do not fit in with their wives plans. The wife must fit in with her husband's plans. His plans must fit in with the Lord's plans in extending the Kingdom of God.

Col 3:18-19, Wives, adapt yourselves to your husbands; that is your Christian duty. Husbands give your wives much love; never treat them harshly.

It is clear in the scripture that God has given to the husband the Lordship and priesthood of his family. His wife is to help him minister the Word of the Lord Jesus Christ to his children and to the world. His ministry is to wash his wife with God's Word to set her apart and cleanse her. Just as Christ is bringing His church into greater glory, so husbands bring your wives continually to greater glory through your priesthood.

WIVES ORDER

As wives operate in their divine order, their submissive role shows the church and its reverence, admiration, obedience and love toward the Lord Jesus. This is of utmost importance to God. Lucifer's rebellion was a usurping of God's order in the universe. Through the Lord Jesus Christ, God is restoring His order and bringing all things in submission to Him. Marriage in God's order clearly demonstrates to the principalities and powers that His way is immutable.

Submission goes far beyond outward duties. When a wife looks on her husband, she is looking on the office God ordained. As she acknowledges THAT apart from his failures, weakness in the flesh and personality or even "good things" of his natural person, she will immediately experience God's blessing on her, because she is acknowledging the office that God ordained for her to submit to. When a wife fails to submit, she usurps her husband's office and stops the blessing of God. God is displeased!

I Cor 11:3, But I wish you to understand that, while every man has Christ for his Head, woman's head is man, as Christ's Head is God.

In the Christian marriage, wives properly related to their husbands in the Kingdom Business are invaluable to him. Without them, he could not be a husband. He could not multiply; he would not be complete. A wife's place is to be a "help fit for him" and heirs together of the inheritance in life that God has prepared for you.

So-called "good" marriages in the world are operated by the good side of the tree of the knowledge of Good and Evil. Many so-called "good" marriages in Christianity are also operated by the good side of the tree of eh knowledge of Good and Evil. There is no difference. It is still run by the natural mind. Neither one shows the glory of God. Both could operate if God did not exist, or if the Holy Spirit was not around.

Marriage under the Lordship of Jesus Christ operates in the authority of His Kingdom. The power of the Kingdom is at work in the marriage as submission is made to God's order. This type of a marriage could not operate without God's power. Could your marriage operate without God?

Kingdom marriages demonstrate God's power through submission. The husband submitted to the Lord Jesus and the wife submitted to her husband. God honors such a marriage with His power and blessing. He will sustain it with His immeasurable love.

ASSIGNMENTS

LESSON 3 ASSIGNMENT 1

If single, this is a good lesson in preparation for marriage, and important information for married couples. Does this bring up any issues that might need to be dealt with that could be affected by what you have learned about breakthrough dominion within the family. What are some specific action steps you can take to make some changes in the family dynamic that will increase effectiveness when moving forward and taking dominion in your own lives?

LESSON 3 ASSIGNMENT 2

Copy and Paste your SMART goal here and update based on what you have learned.

Lesson 4: Children and Family

INTRODUCTION

GOD'S KINGDOM ORDER FOR CHILDREN

There is no comparison between the world's concepts concerning children and God's dynamic plan. Let's take a look at God's reason for children.

Just as man's reason for being under the Lordship of Jesus Christ is to multiply, replenish, take dominion and subdue, in short, to extend the Kingdom. So, the woman's purpose is to help and enter into his purpose and ministry. The children become instruments of dominion in their parent's hands. In this, they glorify God in His purposes and confirm their reason for being.

Children in God's Kingdom are looked upon as a reward from God. They are the result of the command of God to multiply.

> *Ps 127:3-5, Lo children are an heritage of the Lord; and the fruit of the womb is His reward. As arrows are in the hand of a mighty man; so are children of the youth. Happy is the man that hath his quiver full of them.*

Parents authorize children through the act of love, the act of re-uniting and becoming one flesh.

Gen 2:24, Therefore shall a man leave his father and his mother and shall cleave to his wife, and they shall be one flesh.

Multiplication comes when the rib that was taken from the man's side is re-united (becomes one flesh) with man, from whom it was taken. When the church (Christ's bride) is united to Him in one accord, the Lod adds daily to the church.

Acts 2:46-47, and they, continuing daily with one accord in the temple, and breaking bread from house to house, did eat their meat with gladness and singleness of heart, Praising God and having favor with all the people. And the Lord added to the church daily such as should be saved.

GOD'S ORDER IN THE FAMILY

Children are to submit, obey and honor their father and mother as the ones who authorized their life.

Eph 6:1-3, Children, obey your parents in the Lord; for this is right. Honor thy father and

> *mother, which is the first commandment with promise, that it may be well with thee, and that thou mayest live long on the earth.*

This promise connected with obedience to parents is a long and prosperous life. To a child in a Christian family under the Lordship of Jesus Christ, it is his first experience with authority, submission and obedience to the Lord represented in the joint office of father and mother. Thus, it is the most important training of his entire life. How he is trained and in what order or disorder he learns, determines how he will submit to the Lord Jesus Christ later on or how a wife will submit to her husband.

> *Prov 22:6, Train up a child in the way he should go; and when he is old, he will not depart from it.*

Why won't he depart? Because he has seen the goodness of God in the land of the living.

> *Ps 27:13, I had fainted, unless I had believed to see the goodness of the Lord in the land of the living.*

Ours is the only read authority for child rearing. We have the God-given responsibility to train our children. How should we teach? By example, by word, and by scriptural discipline. The average child reaches 17 years of age, he has watched an average of 20 hours of TV a week. He goes to public school six hours a day, 185 days per year for 12 of the most impressionable years of his life. Who is training our children? Subjects are being taught as though God does not exist.

To a father, our heavenly Father gives the opportunity of experiencing His own fatherhood. All earthly parenthood is channeled down the same chain of command. God, Lord Jesus, father, mother, children in that order.

Parents must love their children. How? Self-sacrificially. With God's love. We love them by the Word of God.

> *Deut. 6:6-7, "And these words, which I command thee this day, shall be in thine heart; And thou shalt teach them diligently unto thy children, and shalt talk of them when thou sittest in thine house and when thou walkest by the way, and when thou liest down, and when thou rises up."*

The greatest way to love your children is to teach them God's word that they may live productive lives, purposed in God's command to extend His kingdom. They must live in the reality of Christ's commission to make disciples of all nations. Then the teaching of God's word has purpose in their lives. They must know the relevancy of this commission in every area of their life (education, business, home, government).

All His abilities, energy, and learning must be directed toward and for the purpose of the Lord Jesus Christ. Many Christian parent's guide their children and encourage their energies toward holding positions in secular life to support their families and experience the "good life!" What about God's reason for every saved person including our children?

ARROWS IN THE QUIVER

In the family of God, children are weapons and hep in the work of the Father. In the old days, people lived on farms and the more children, the better. In some places this is still true. In the days of Israel, a man's sons were his defense. When an elder in Israel came to the gate to meet with him enemies, his sons were there to back him up.

> *Ps. 127:5, Happy is the man that hath his quiver full of them; they shall not be ashamed, but they shall speak with the enemies in the gate.*

It is vain to raise children and turn them over to the world when they reach a certain age. This is not God's plan. They will always be a part of the same family of God. They have been taught to live under the Lordship of Jesus Christ wherever they are stewarding their talents, reaping the benefits of their work, giving to advance the kingdom, and brining many more brothers and sisters into the family.

GOD'S PURPOSE FOR FAMILIES

GOD'S PURPOSE IN MULTIPLYING IS TO MAKE FAMILIES:

> *Ps 107:41-43, yet setteth he the poor on high from affliction, and maketh him families like a flock. The righteous shall see it and rejoice and all iniquity shall step her mouth. Whoso is wise, and will observe these things, even shall understand the loving kindness of the Lord.*

God brings us out of darkness into the kingdom of His dear Son. He brings us into His family It is not His will to leave us in the same cultural setting in which He found us. He brings us into Lordship and the delegated authority of His Kingdom. When the righteous begin to rejoice and live in God's order, all lawlessness will stop her mouth.

Ps 68:5-6, A father of the fatherless, and a judge of the widows, is God in His holy habitation. God setteth the solitary in families; He bringeth out those which are bound with chains; but he rebellious dwell in a dry land.

God's Attitude Toward Those Who Would Afflict a Fatherless Child

Ex 22:22-24, ye shall not afflict any widow or fatherless child. If thou afflict them in any wise and they cry at all unto Me, I will surely hear their cry. And My wrath shall wax hot, and I will kill you with the sword; and your wives shall be widows and your children fatherless.

God's attitude toward children without fathers or wives without husbands is that they would come to Him. He has extreme mercy on people that have been cast out. He exhorts us to bring them into His family to be cared for.

Mal. 3:5, And I will come near to you to judgement; and I will be a swift witness against the sorcerers, and against the adulterers, and against the false swearers, and against those that oppress the hireling in his wages ,the widow and the fatherless and that turn aside the stranger from his right and fear not Me saith the Lord of hosts.

GOD'S COMMANDMENTS TO CHILDREN

TO REVERENCE AND FEAR PARENTS

Lev. 19:3, Ye shall fear every man his mother and his father and keep my Sabbaths; I am the Lord.

RESPECT THE OLD MAN

Lev. 19:32, Thou shalt rise up before the hoary head and honor the face of the old man.

Remember the Word of Godly parents, as they have taught God's Word

Prov 6:20, My son, keep thy father's commandment and forsake not the law of thy mother. Bind them continually upon thine heart and tie them about thy neck. When thou goest, it shall lead thee; when thou sleepest, it shall keep thee; and when thou wakest, it shall talk with thee.

GOD COMMANDS US TO CORRECT OUR CHILDREN

If you love them, you correct them

Prov 13:24: He that spareth the rod hateth his own son; but he that loveth him chatiseneth him betimes.

Don't spare because he cries

Prov. 19:18, Chasten thy son while there is hope, and let not thy soul spare for is crying.

DON'T OVER-CORRECT OR TEASE IN YOUR CORRECTION

Eph. 6:4, You fathers, again, must not goad your children to resentment, but give them the instructions and the correction, which belong to a Christian upbringing.

GOD'S ATTITUDE TOWARD REBELLIOUS CHILDREN

PERSON WHO HITS FATHER OR MOTHER WORTHY OF DEATH

Ex. 21:15, 17, And he that smiteth his father, or his mother shall be surely put to death; and he that curseth his father or his mother, shall surely be put to death.

INCORRIGIBLE SONS PUT TO DEATH

Deut. 21:18-21, If a man has a stubborn and rebellious son, which will not obey the voice of his father, or the voice of his mother and that, when they have chastened him, will not hearken unto them. Then shall his father and his mother lay hold on him, and bring him out unto the elders of his city and unto the gate of his place; And they shall say unto the elders of his city, This our son is stubborn and rebellious, he will not obey our voice; he is a glutton and a drunkard. And all the men of his city shall stone him with stone, that he die, so shalt thou put evil away from among you; and all Israel hear and fear.

CURSING OF PARENTS DRAWS THE JUDGEMENT OF GOD

Prov. 30:11, 17, There is a generation that curseth their father and doth not bless their mother. The eye that mocketh at his father and despiseth to obey his mother, the ravens of the valley shall pick it out and the young eagles shall eat it.

REWARDS OF CORRECTION

Prov 29:17, Correct thy son and he shall give thee rest, yea he shall give delight unto thy soul.

1 Peter 2:9, But ye are a chosen generation, a royal priesthood a holy nation, a peculiar people; that ye should shew forth the praises of Him who

> *hath called you out of darkness into His marvelous light.*

Each father should realize the only reason for his marriage is to extend the Kingdom of God and to complete the mandate commanded by God to Adam to take dominion over the earth and subdue it. We accomplish this through God's Holy Spirit operating in God's orderly arrangement in the family.

When families are moving together under the Lordship of Jesus Christ, their intent is His Kingdom first and that's why they exist. They're able to invest time and energy together for God's purpose. When everything is under His Lordship, everything becomes available and alive to His control. Arrows are being shot in different directions. Some perhaps overseas in a team, some in business, some to school. All for the purpose of taking dominion and subduing. Each are under Christ's Lordship.

Assignments

LESSON 4 ASSIGNMENT 1

Write about your family dynamic growing up. Did you have both parents? Siblings? Corporal punishment or other correction. What views have you adopted based on that, and do you see any differences in this lesson that maybe were taught incorrectly or do you see some areas where you might need to make some changes in your current family unit?

LESSON 4 ASSIGNMENT 2

If you do not have children, this is a great lesson in preparation for when/if you choose to have them in the future, but overall helps understand the fullness of the word "dominion." If you do have children, write about your family unit and how this lesson has offered any new information that you can apply within your own family unit?

Lesson 5 Work, A Vehicle of Dominion

INTRODUCTION

Gen 2:15, And the Lord God took the man and put him into the Garden of Eden to dress it and to keep it.

The word and ministry that God gave Adam before the fall was to tend the Garden of Eden.

Ex. 20:8-9, Remember the Sabbath day, to keep it holy. Six days shalt thou labor and do all thy work.

Work finds its purpose in the original mandate God gave to Adam.

Gen. 1:28, And God blessed them, and God said unto them, "Be fruitful and multiply and replenish the earth, and subdue it; and have dominion over the fish and over the fowl of the air, and over every living thing that moveth upon the earth.

Work obviously continued after the fall with man knowing the frustration of sin in his calling. With the fall came a curse on man's work, but work is not a curse.

Gen. 3:17-19, And unto Adam He said, Because thou has hearkened unto the voice of thy wife, and hast eaten of the tree, of which I commanded thee, saying, Thou shalt not eat of it; cursed is the ground for thy sake; in sorrow shalt thou eat of it all the days of thy life; Thorns also and thistles shall it bring forth to thee; and thou shalt eat the herb of the field; In the sweat of thy face shalt thou eat bread, till thou return unto the ground; for out of it wast thou taken; for dust thou art and unto dust shalt thou return.

WORK IN THE KINGDOM

In the Kingdom of the Lord Jesus Christ, work takes on a new dimension All work has purpose. It is a vehicle that God has ordained at creation to replenish the earth, subdue (or work) it, and have dominion. The Gospel of the Kingdom must be preached in every nation. Work has a very important part in this commission. Through the tithe, first fruits, and freewill offerings, God's program for dominion is more than financed.

Matt. 24:14, And this gospel of the Kingdom will be proclaimed throughout the earth as a testimony to all nations; and then the end will come.

Matt. 28:18-20, All power in Heaven and earth has been given to Me. You then are to go and make disciples of all the nations and baptize them int eh name of the Father and of the Son and of the Holy Spirit. Teach them to observe all that I have commanded you and remember, I am with you always, even to the end of the world.

GOD'S WORD STRESSES THE DIGNITY AND IMPORTANT OF WORK

Prov. 13:11, Wealth gotten by vanity shall be diminished; but he that gathereth by labor shall increase.

Through the agency of work. God gives to man an opportunity to develop his potential, mentally, physically and emotionally. When Jesus is Lord of a person's work, he becomes diligent as he works as unto the Lord and for His Lord's purposes.

Prov. 12:24, The hand of the diligent shall bear rule: but the slothful shall be under tribute.

Prov. 13:4, The soul of the sluggard desireth, and hath nothing; but the soul of the diligent shall be made fat.

Prov. 22:29, Seest thou a man diligent in his business? He shall stand before kings; he shall not stand before mean men.

The world's idea of work does not extend past personal need or desire. Men work to eat and pay bills for self.

Most Christians see their work separate and secular, thus their responsibility before God is perhaps a few hours a week, when their work takes at least 40 hours per week. Most of the wages go to pay their bills and perhaps 10% goes to the kingdom. They have the idea that they and those who have a "MINISTRY" are different species. They don't realize that their reason for work is the same as the preacher's reason for preaching; that is to extend the kingdom of Jesus Christ.

> *Col. 3:22-25, Servants, obey in all things your masters according to the flesh; not in eye service, as men pleasers but in singleness of heart, fearing God; and whatever you do, do it heartily as to the Lord and not unto men. Knowing that of the Lord ye shall receive the reward of the inheritance; for ye serve the Lord Christ. Bu he that doeth wrong shall receive for the wrong which he hath done; and there is no respect of persons.*

DO ALL UNDER THE LORDSHIP OF JESUS CHRIST

> *Col 3:17, And whatsoever ye do in word or deed to all in the name of the Lord Jesus, giving thanks to God and the Father by Him.*

> *Eccl. 2:11 Then I looked on all the works that my hands had wrought, and on the labor that I had labored to do; and behold, all was vanity and vexation of spirits, and there was not profit under the sun.*

Because of work without purpose beyond self, family, need and desire, the frustrations of today's marketplace cause men to seek to escape from work or into work. They become play oriented and can't wait for the weekend to get into the motorhome and head for escape country. On the other hand, some become work-a-holics, spending 16 hours a day on the job, becoming obsessed with their work. Each of these extremes are void of satisfaction or fulfillment. People in this dilemma are usually people that add drugs and alcohol to their unreal trek. Anything but responsibility, result is chronic discontent, self-righteousness, anger, impatience, symptoms of human beings out of touch with reality. Culture becomes radically dislocated. Spiritual poverty makes hypocrisy and out-ward appearances more important that life itself. Man should enjoy work and delight in it. ON the contrary, however, escape formwork is a common desire among men.

> *Eccles. 2:17-23, Therefore I hated life, because the work that is wrought under the sun is grievous unto me; for all is vanity and vexation of spirit. Yea I hated all my labor which I had taken under the sun; because I should leave it unto the man that shall be after me. And who knoweth whether he shall be a wise man or a fool? Yet shall he have rule over all of my labor wherein I have labored, and wherein I have showed myself wise under the sun. This is also Vanity. Therefore, I went about to cause my heart to despair of all the labor which I took under the sun. For there is a man whose labor is in wisdom and in knowledge and in equity. Yet to a man that hath not labored therein shall he leave It for his portion. This also is vanity and a great evil. For what hat a man of all his labor, and of the vexation of his heart, wherein he hath labored under the sun? For all his days are sorrows, and his travail grief; yea, his ear taketh not rest in the night. This is also vanity.*

The lure of Marxism and similar faiths is their declaration that man is fettered to work and must be freed from it. More recently, the claim has been made that work can be abolished by automation, and a freed society is freed from work. The great contradiction here is that work is a man's calling, yet in working, he realizes that God's curse it on his work. From this he tries to escape.

GOD'S ORDER: THROUGH THE VEHICLE OF BUSINESS

WHERE IS THIS CONTRADICTION MANIFESTED?

1. In man's being
2. In man's society

Man knows in the depths of his being that work is his destiny under God. It is his self-realizations well as his calling and that a man's manhood is essentially tied to his ability to work and his development in terms of work.

Socialist dreamers capitalize on man's frustration. They offer man a utopia in which the curse has supposedly been abolished by the abolition of a certain class of men who are called the "EXPLOITERS." Somehow, paradise will then be restored. According to Marx, man will be freed from the curse on man and work by the

Socialist paradise in which the division of labor will disappear. This philosophy is an effort of man to lift himself out of the effects of the fall by his own efforts.

Because this cannot work, society is affected by the moving away from reality to appearances. The poor may suffer from reality, but that is better than suffering from make believe. Since the world is maintained in its social and cultural order and progress by work, not make believe, a world in which make believe gains predominance is a world moving toward collapse. As we take a look at today's idols – rock stars, movie actors and actresses, we realize that our society is moving rapidly into an unreal mentality that hides itself in television, theatre, and sporting events. They live vicariously in the grandstands, not really participating in real life.

THIS KIND OF PHILOSOPHY BREEDS IDLENESS AND SLOTHFULNESS

A. Of a sluggard who desires but has nothing

Prov. 13:4, The soul of the sluggard desireth and hath nothing but the soul of the diligent shall be made fat.

B. Of a slothful person who wastes his time and others

Prov. 18:9, He also that is slothful in his work is brother to him that is a great waster.

C. Of a slothful person who because of it suffers hunger

Prov 19:15, Slothfulness casteth into a deep sleep; and an idle soul shall suffer hunger.

D. And that this desire of a slothful person will kill him.

Prov. 21:25, the desire of the slothful killeth him; for his hands refuse to labor.

KINGDOM WORD ETHICS PROVIDE MOTIVATION FOR DILIGENCE

1 Thes. 4:11-12, And that ye study to be quiet, and to do your own business, and to work with your own hands and we commanded you. That ye may walk honestly toward them that are without and that ye may have lack of nothing.

Prov. 22:29, Seest though a man diligent in his business? He shall stand before kings; he shall not stand before mean men.

> *Prov. 21:5, The thoughts of the diligent tend only to plenteousness; but of everyone that is hasty only to want.*

> *2 Thes. 3:10-12, For even when we were with you, this we commanded you, that is any would not work, neither should he eat. For we hear that there are some which walk among you disorderly, working not at all, but are busybodies. Now them that are such, we command and exhort by our Lord Jesus Christ, that which quietness they work, and eat their own bread.*

God's plan for work under the Lordship of Jesus Christ has motivation that has a great effect on the way one performs. He sees it as a tool of his ministry, thus his desk, tractor and position become his pulpit for ministering Jesus Christ. His work and craftmanship is consistently moving toward greater efficiency, because his time, energy and skills are all pointed toward God's purposes and at God's hand he will receive the reward. Work, therefore, becomes a platform that God uses to exalt His people into a higher position in life and a greater place of authority for the Kingdom's sake.

CONCLUSION

God has given man work as a means to bring all of life's energies, provision, time, talent, and productivity under the Lordship of Jesus Christ; and through Him, His Kingdom, and His orderly arrangement of authority, take dominion over the whole earth, subduing all things under His feet and making the earth His foot stool.

Assignments

LESSON 5 ASSIGNMENT 1

What does the dominion mandate in your work mean to you? How does walking in the dominion mandate change the way you view your job? Your ministry?

LESSON 5 ASSIGNMENT 2

What are the goals you have and plans to step into to fulfill your SMART goal to walk in the dominion mandate? How does it affect your work, your job or your ministry?

Lesson 6
The Church, A Vehicle of Dominion

INTRODUCTION

HEAVENLY HEADSHIP IN EARTHLY BODIES

> *2 Cor 4:7, But we have this treasure in fragile earthen pots in order that the surpassing greatness of the power maybe seen to be God's and not to come from us.*

The ascension into the heavens by the Lord Jesus, our King, procures for us authority over the earth realm. Out of this authority, we act as ambassadors form the Kingdom of God.

> *2 Cor. 5:20, Now then we are ambassadors for Christ, as though God did beseech you by us; we pray you in Christ's stead, be ye reconciled to God.*

We bring the message of reconciliation to the captives of the earth and declare that Jesus defeated all the enemies of mankind.

The Church is the Most Potent of the Dominion Vehicles

> *Eph 2:6 (Weymouth), ...raised us up with Him from the dead, and enthroned us with Him in the heavenly realms as being in Christ Jesus.*

This is where our authority lies

Eph 1:21 (Weymouth), it is above all other governments and authority and power and dominion, and every title of sovereignty used either in this age or in the age to come.

This gives the church ultimate authority and power and dominion, and every title of sovereignty used ether in this age or in the age to come.

THE ASCENSION PROCURES HEAVENLY WEAPONS (GIFTS)

ASCENSION GIFTS – GOD'S GOVERNMENTAL GIFTS

Eph. 4:7-16, But unto every one of us is given grace according to the measure of the gift of Christ. Wherefore he saith, When He ascended up on high, He led captivity captive, and gave gifts unto men. Now that he ascended, what is it but that He also descended first into the lower parts of the earth? He that descended is the same also that ascended up far above all heavens, that He might fill all things. And He gave some apostles, some prophets; and some, evangelists and some pastors and teachers; for the perfecting of the saints for the work of the ministry of the edifying of the body of

Christ. Till we all come in the unity of the faith and of the knowledge of the Son of God, unto a perfect man, unto the measure of the stature of the fulness of Christ; That we henceforth be no more children, tossed to and fro and carried about with every wind of doctrine, by the sleight of men and cunning craftiness, whereby they lie and wait to deceive, but speaking the truth in love, may grow up into Him in all things, which is the head, even Christ; from whom the whole body fitly joined together and compacted by that which every joint supplieth according to the effectual working in the measure of every part, maketh increase of the body unto the edifying of itself in love.

THE CHURCH PROVIDES ENVIRONMENT FOR DOMINION

Christ's body, the Church, provides the environment in which His commission to make disciples of all nations, is accomplished.

THE KEYS OF THE KINGDOM OPEN HEAVEN'S DOOR

Matt. 1:18, 19, And I say also unto thee that though art Peter, ad upon this rock I will build My Church and the gates of hell shall not prevail against it. And I will give unto thee the keys of the Kingdom of Heaven' and whatsoever though shalt bind on earth shall be bound in heaven' and whatsoever thou shalt look on earth shall be loosed in heaven.

Matt. 6:9-10, After this manger therefore pray ye, Our Father which art in Heaven, Hallowed by Thy Name. Thy Kingdom come; Thy will be done in earth as it is in heaven.

THE CHURCH IS GIVEN POWER FOR DOMINION

Jesus Christ gives the keys of the Kingdom of heaven that His Kingdom may be established through the Church.

Mark 16:15-20 (Phillips), You must go out to the whole world and proclaim the gospel to every creature. He who believes it and is baptized will be saved, but he who disbelieves it will be condemned. These signs shall follow those who believe: they will drive out evil spirits in My Name; they will speak with new tongues; they will pick up snakes and if they drink any poison it will do them no harm; they will lay their hands on the sick and they will recover. After He spoke these words to them, the Lord Jesus was taken up into Heaven and was enthroned at the right hand of God. They went out and preached everywhere.

The Lord worked with them, confirming their messages by the signs that followed.

THE HOLY SPIRIT PROVIDES DYNAMICS FOR DOMINION

The New Testament church is a living organism brought into being y the death, burial and resurrection of Jesus Christ. He is the head of His body, the Church. The Church, made up of Jewish and Gentile believers, is God's vehicle for dominion and restoration of God's Kingdom order to the earth. When the Lord Jesus ascended to the throne, to sit at the right hand of the Authority on High, He sent back the Holy Spirit to the Church to empower it. Along with the power, or dunamis, came God's order to house the power. To govern God's Church, He sent governing gifts: Apostles, Prophets, Evangelists, Pastors and Teachers.

I Cor. 12:27-31, Now ye are the body of Christ and members in particular. And God hath set some in the church first apostles, secondarily prophets, thirdly teachers after that miracles, then gifts of healings, helps governments, diversities of tongues. Are all Apostles? Are all Prophets? Are all Teachers? Are all workers of miracles? Have all the gifts of healing? Do all speak with tongues? Do all interpret? But covet earnestly the best gifts; and yet she I you a more excellent way.

The purpose of these governing offices is the building up, the training, and the administering of the activities of the Church.

RESPONSIBILITY TOWARD

GIVE DOUBLE HONOR TO ELDERS THAT RULE WELL

1 Tim. 5:17, Let the elders that rule well be counted worthy of double honor, especially they who labor in the word and doctrine.

Remember to follow the example of the eldership, considering their reward

Heb 13:7, Remember them which have the rule over you, who have spoken unto you the word of God; whose faith follow, considering the end of their conversations.

Those who watch over you are responsible unto god for your souls. This demands submission on your part. God will avenge disobedience.

Heb 13:17, Obey them that have the rule over you, and submit yourselves; for they watch for your souls as they that much give account, that they

may do it with joy and not with grief; for that is unprofitable for you.

1 Thes. 5:12, 13, And we beseech you, brethren, to know them which labor among you and are over you in the Lord and admonish you. And to esteem them very highly in love for their work's sake. And be at peace among yourselves.

Those who labor in the word are to be esteem them very highly in love and honor. Why? Because of their responsibility before God for what they teach you.

James 3:1, my brethren, be not many masters, knowing that we shall receive the greater condemnation.

God's charge to shepherds is to take willing oversight of the flock. Taking from their example. The Chief Shepard, the Lord Jesus Christ. He is not a hireling.

1 Pet. 5:1-5, The elders which are among you, I exhort, who am also an elder, and a witness of the sufferings of Christ, and also a partaker of the glory that shall be revealed. Feed the flock of God, which is among you, taking oversight thereof, not by constraint, but willingly, not for filthy lucre, but of a ready mind. Neither as being lords over

God's heritage, but being examples to the flock, and when the Chief Shepard shall appear, ye shall receive a crown of glory that fadeth not away. Likewise, ye younger, submit yourselves unto the elder. Yea all of you be subject one to another and be clothed with humility for God resisteth the proud, and giveth grace to the humble.

EXERCISE OF APOSTOLIC AUTHORITY

OUR AUTHORITY

2 Cor. 10:8-11, For though I should boast somewhat more of our authority, which the Lord hath given us for edification and not be ashamed, that I may not seem as if I would terrify you by letters. For His letters, say they are weighty and powerful; but his bodily presence is weak, and his speech is contemptible. Let such a one think this, that such as we are in word by letters when we are absent, such will we be also in deed when we are present.

Paul's authority challenged by the Corinthian church. He affirms that he is not only able to exercise his authority in his letter, but he is able to exercise it indeed when he got thee.

PAUL'S POWER WAS GIVEN TO BUILD UP...NOT DESTROY

> *2 Cor. 13:10, Therefore I write these things being absent, lest being present I should use sharpness according to the power which the Lord hath given me to edification and not destruction.*

POWER TO CHASTISE

> *1 Cor. 4:14-21, I write not these things to shame you, but as my beloved sons, I warn you; For though ye have ten thousand instructors in Christ, yet have ye not many fathers; for in Christ Jesus I have begotten you through the gospel. Wherefore I beseech you, be ye followers of me. For this cause, have I sent unto you Timotheus, who is my beloved son, and faithful in the Lord, who shall bring you into remembrances of my ways which be in Christ, as I teach everywhere in every church. Now some are puffed up as though I would not come to you. But I will come to you shortly, if the Lord will, and will know, not the speech of them which are puffed up but the power. For the Kingdom of God is not in word but in power. What will ye? Shall I come unto you with a rod or in love and in meekness?*

The power that the apostle had could be chastisement to the rebellious.

Instructions to not associate with those who are walking disorderly

2 Thes 3:6-7, Now we command you, brethren, in the name of our Lord Jesus Christ, that ye withdraw yourselves from every brother that walketh disorderly and not after the tradition which he received of us. For yourselves know how ye ought to follow us, for we behaved not ourselves disorderly among you.

2 Thes. 3:14-15, And if any man obey not our word by this epistle, note that man, and have no company with him that he may be ashamed. Yet count him not as an enemy but admonish him as a brother.

EXAMPLES OF APOSTOLIC AUTHORITY

PETER EXERCISED THE POWER TO DISCERN MEN'S HEARTS.

Acts 5:1-11, But a certain man names Ananias, with Sapphira his wife sold a possession. And kept back part of the price, his wife also being privy to it, and brought a certain part, and laid it at the apostles' feet. But Peter said, Ananias, why hath Satan filled thine heart to lie to the Holy Ghost, and to keep back part of the price of the land?

While it remained, was it not tine own? And after it was sold, was it not in thine own power? Why hast thou conceived this thing in thine heart? Thou hast not lied unto men but unto God. Ananias hearing these words, ell down and gave up the ghost; and great fear came on all them that heart these things. And the young men rose, wound him up and carried him out and buried him. And it was about the space of three hours after, when his wife, not knowing what was done, came in. And Peter answered unto her," Tell me whether ye sold the land for so much?" And she said, "Yea for so much." Then Peter said unto her, "How is it that ye have agreed together to tempt the Spirit of the Lord? Behold the feet of them which have buried thy husband are at the door and shall carry thee out". Then fell she down straightway at his feet and yielded up the ghost; and the young men came in and found her dead and carried her forth, buried her by her husband. And great fear came upon all the church and upon as many as heard these things.

POWER TO BLIND – GOD BACKS UP WORD SPOKEN BY PAUL

Acts 13:6-12, And when they had gone through the isle unto Paphos, they found a certain sorcerer, a false prophet, a Jew, whose name was

> *Bar-Jesus which was with the deputy of the country Sergius Paulus, a prudent man; who called for Barnabas an Saul, and desired to hear the word of God. But Eluymas the sorcerer (for so is his name by interpretation) withstood them, seeking to turn away the deputy from the faith. Then Saul (who also is called Paul) filled with the Holy Ghost, set his eyes on him and said, "O full of all subtlety and all mischief, thou child of the devil, thou enemy of all righteousness, wilt thou not cease to pervert the right ways of the Lord? And now, behold, the hand of the Lord is upon thee, and thou shalt be blind, not seeing the sun for a season. And immediately there fell on him a mist and a darkness; and he went about seeking some to lead him by the hand. Then the deputy when he saw what was done, believed, being astonished at the doctrine of the Lord.*

God has given to the church all she needs to carry out His purposes in the earth and to prepare the earth for the King. His power, by the Holy Spirit is constantly drawing men and women out of darkness into His light and confirming the Word of His disciples.

Jesus commission to us is to go and make disciples of all nations. In so doing, He is inheriting the nations and the kingdoms of this world are becoming the kingdom of God and His Christ.

> *Rev 11:15, And the seventh angel sounded; and there were great voices in heaven saying, "The kingdoms of this world are become the kingdoms of our Lord and of His Christ, and He hall reign for ever and ever.*

> *Ps 2:8, Ask of Me and I shall give thee the heathen for thine inheritance, and the uttermost parts of the earth for thy possession.*

> *Dan 7:27, And the Kingdome and dominion and the greatness of the kingdom under the whole heaven shall be given to the people of the saints of the Most High, whose kingdom is an everlasting kingdom and all dominions shall serve and obey Him.*

Assignments

LESSON 6 ASSIGNMENT 1

Copy and paste your updated SMART goal from Lesson 3 here and update it based on what you have learned and include progress you have made throughout the course.

LESSON 6 ASSIGNMENT 2

Write an essay of what you have learned in this course. Describe how the Dominion Mandate in those in the Old Testament, Jesus in the New, give us examples of how to walk it out in every area of life: marriage, children, family, work, church/ministry and what if anything you want to do to walk in dominion more fully.

After Words

Note: The following looks like it is not a part of this teaching but were some typed pages at the end and it appears to only be a portion as it ends mid-sentence.

The Law was given in the arrangement of angels because a fallen angel (Satan) brought the nature of angels into mankind through the disobedience of Adam. The tree of the knowledge of good and evil was never meant for man to eat of. Man was not designed to live in the knowing of good and evil. That tree was in the disposition of angels and the fallen angels became lawless and the same lawless nature was deposited in man. The law was given to curb the lawlessness of man. It was never given to crate righteousness, which could come by faith alone. It is that killing nature that was the posture within the Jewish leaders that killed Stephen in Acts 7:53. That also was the spirit that killed Abel by his brother Cain.

Satan knew by deceiving man into partaking of the fruit of the knowing of good and evil in direct disobedience to God's command that holding this knowledge in the spirit of disobedience would bring condemnation and death upon the creation of God. The knowing of good and evil without the obedience and the union with the Father would bring about a race that the selfish self for walk we call the flesh. In the 7th chapter of Romans, the Apostle Paul describes this conflict in man.

> *Rom. 7:14-25, for we have known that the law is spiritual and I am fleshly sold by the sin for that which I work, I do not acknowledge, for not what I will, this I practice, but what I had, this I do. And if what I do not will, this I do, I consent to the law that it is good. And now it is no longer I that work it, but the sin dwelling in me. For I have known that there doth not dwell in me, that is, in my flesh, good. For to will is present with me, and to work that which is right I do not find. For the good that I will, I do not; but the evil that I do not will, this I practice. And if what I do not will, this I do, it is no longer I that work it, but the sin that is dwelling in me. I find then this law, that when I desire to do what is right, with me the evil is present. For I delight in the law of God according to the inward man. And I behold another law in my members warring against the law of my mind and bringing me into captivity to the law of the sin that is in my members. A wretched man I am, who shall deliver me out of the body of this death? I thank Go, through Jesus Christ our Lord; so then, I myself indeed with the mind to serve the law of God, and with the flesh, the law of sin.*

The knowledge of good and evil is being played out and has formed a system called "the world." The enemies of God are the world system, the flesh and through mortal bodies. What a promise! God can make alive everything that comes to us, in action, in motive, in wisdom, and that He is, is brought to us by the Holy Spirit. As He is, so are we on the earth. The Holy Spirit can bring that Life to us who believe. As we move in faith, the Holy Spirit is activated on our behalf in the name of Jesus. We need not fear for in Him all the promises of God are; Yes, and so be It.

DNA -THE SACRED SPIRAL

DNA deoxyribonucleic acid, in the DNA spiral is all of history that our ancestry has lived on the earth. It has been passed down. Family characteristics; emotional and physical, are held within this spiral. Much of our lives are influenced by some degree by the past, but not only ours but by our ancestry. The word of God indicates this when it speaks of "generational curses," the "sins of the fathers visited on the children up to the 4th generation" and the fathers have eaten sour grapes and the children's teeth are on edge. When repentance was made it asked for the forgiveness of the fathers and the nation. Each person on the earth has the power of choice to make a decision.

None of our decisions stand alone. To some degree, it changes the whole world. The more authority that a person has, the greater affect he has on the entire world. To understand how this power works and how principalities and powers work in this and we must know the purpose of the principalities and powers. The word tells us they were created by Jesus and for him. Their intention in the beginning was to aid Adam in his rule and dominion in the creation that was made for mankind as we know Him today. His mind was at full capacity. His imagination, will, emotion, all was in a state of innocence. He had union and fellowship with his Father and Creator. The devil and sin came in through disobedience. His facility began to corrupt and dissipate. The only fruit that he had to eat was the knowledge of good and evil. This was the beginning of the world system. A world that was built and rebuilt by the mind of the flesh. The Word tells us the three things that are our enemy are the world (the fallen nature of the world), the flesh and the devil. The principalities and power were and have been educated by these forces.

These entities are in touch with the total facility of man. Man's mind (intellect, imagination, feeling, consciousness) both conscience and sub-conscience (man's will, emotions). How man relates to others. Society and its formation. They have formed belief systems and cultures and have held masses of people captive for generations.

RELATION TO FAMILIES AND GENERATIONS

How does the sin of ancestry relate to us? If we look back on our father, grandfather, great-grandfather. Whether we are aware of it or not, we have been affected or rather infected. Our body, soul and spirit have within it the sins of the family. The characteristics, the weaknesses, character flaws proneness in areas are all three We did not ask for them, they are there just the same. To show this in scripture, we see the sins of the fathers are visited upon the children of the third and the fourth generation of the fathers have eaten sour grapes and the children's teeth are on edge. There are many more indicators that this is true. I believe that is why the prayer of repentance is not only offered for what has happened recently, but what has happened in the past.

In Nehemiah prayer, in Neh. 1:4-11, this was a great prayer from an intercessor. One who understood the gravity or the situation and made intercession for the nation, including his family and generations past. In verse 6, he says for the children of Israel your servants and confess the sins of the children of Israel which we have sinned against you. Both my father's house and I have sinned. First, it recognizes the greatness and the awesomeness of God and His great and tender mercies. Then it confesses and repents and evokes God's mercy and grace on the task ahead of him for the restoration of the wall. There are many prayers that recognize the generational sins and pleads for the gift of repentance.

HOW IS THIS CONNECTED TO THE DNA OF MAN?

Romans 7 gives us the example of how ingrained the nature of sin is in our members. He says they were instruments of unrighteousness in Romans 6 and Romans 7. He likens it to a marriage, the union that Adam made with the knowledge of good and evil in the garden. In the DNA spiral that resides in every cell of our body, is our history and our family tree

> *Rom. 7:22-25, for I delight in the law of God according to the inward man, and I behold another law in my members, warring against the law of my mind, and bringing me into captivity to the law of the sin, that is in my member. A wretched man I am@ Who shall deliver me out of the body of this death? I thank God – through Jesus Christ our Lord; so then, I myself indeed with the mind do serve the law of God, and with the flesh, the law of sin.*

In the history that is in our members constitute our lifetime alone or some of which belongs to our ancestry? There is within our natural members the history of our ancestry. How far it goes back, I don't know, perhaps to Adam and Eve. Perhaps there is residue of many generations that is there. This I know through one man, Adam, corruption entered through an act of disobedience. We call this nature "the flesh." The Bible says, through the apostles Paul, "In my flesh there is no good thing." I also know that in Christ Jesus who the Bible calls, the "second Adam" or "the man from heaven."

> *1 Cor. 15:47-49, The first man is of the earth, earthy; the second man is the Lord form heaven. As is the earthy, such are they also that are earthy; and as is the heavenly, such are they also that are heavenly.*

The heavenly man (Jesus) is the head of the new creation. He was the first born as a man out of the grave after suffering the consequence of our sin and was raised up the dead of another race. The DNA spiral has a new heritage. I now belong to Jesus in the Father. This place I called "In Christ." Now we derive our past and identity from Him and bring forth the fruit of this……..

Made in the USA
San Bernardino, CA
08 June 2020

72933120R00068